Skyscrapers and Towers

Shirley Duke

Rourke
Educational Media

rourkeeducationalmedia.com

Before Reading:

Building Academic Vocabulary and Background Knowledge

Before reading a book, it is important to tap into what your child or students already know about the topic. This will help them develop their vocabulary, increase their reading comprehension, and make connections across the curriculum.

1. *Look at the cover of the book. What will this book be about?*
2. *What do you already know about the topic?*
3. *Let's study the Table of Contents. What will you learn about in the book's chapters?*
4. *What would you like to learn about this topic? Do you think you might learn about it from this book? Why or why not?*
5. *Use a reading journal to write about your knowledge of this topic. Record what you already know about the topic and what you hope to learn about the topic.*
6. *Read the book.*
7. *In your reading journal, record what you learned about the topic and your response to the book.*
8. *After reading the book complete the activities below.*

Content Area Vocabulary
Read the list. What do these words mean?

bedrock
counterweight
debris
deformation
footings
innovate
parapet
rebar
shear
structural supports
structurally sound
substructure
sustainable
torsion

After Reading:

Comprehension and Extension Activity

After reading the book, work on the following questions with your child or students in order to check their level of reading comprehension and content mastery.

1. *Why is a strong foundation important when building a skyscraper?* (Summarize)
2. *What natural elements are considered when building a skyscraper or tower?* (Asking questions)
3. *Have you ever been in a skyscraper? What was it like?* (Text to self connection)
4. *Explain why the outside walls can be made of fragile materials such as glass.* (Infer)
5. *How are skyscrapers today different from ancient buildings?* (Summarize)

Extension Activity

Engineers carefully plan building skyscrapers to ensure the safety of people during natural forces such as earthquakes. Using a variety of materials such as marshmallows, toothpicks, Popsicle sticks, glue, or Legos, create a skyscraper. Think about important parts of constructing a skyscraper, including a strong base and a core. Build a skyscraper and test how it would hold up during an earthquake. Place the structure on a board and shake it. What happened? What parts of the building stayed together? What changes could you make?

Table of Contents

Tall Treasures 4

Powerful Forces. 9

The Building Goes Up 15

Historical Towers. 21

Towers around the World 31

What's New with Skyscrapers?. 41

Timeline 45

Glossary 46

Index. 47

Show What You Know 47

Websites to Visit 47

About the Author 48

The Eiffel Tower is 1,063 feet (324 meters) tall, including the antenna at the top.

Tall Treasures

Look at a picture of any city. Can you tell where it is by the structures that you see?

The Empire State Building stands tall against New York City's skyline. The Eiffel Tower rises above Paris, France. The tilt of the Leaning Tower of Pisa is famous in Italy.

The Leaning Tower of Pisa is now considered to be a work of art. It took nearly two centuries to be completed.

Extremely tall buildings are called skyscrapers because their height makes them appear to reach to the sky.

Towers are not buildings. Buildings have floors with homes or offices in them. A tower is a tall, narrow structure that can be part of a building or stand alone. Bell housings on churches are an example of a tower.

Big Ben is the nickname for the Great Bell of the clock in the tower at the Palace of Westminster in London. It first chimed on May 31, 1859.

Engineers use technology to develop, **innovate**, and create new things, including buildings. They also look for ways to improve technology. Architects design buildings and towers. They draw the plans for buildings and towers and oversee their construction.

Towers have existed for thousands of years. The 11,000-year-old Tower of Jericho, at 38 feet (8.5 meters) tall, is thought to be the first skyscraper in the world. It was built with stone and mud. The ancient Egyptians built the first towers as pyramids. The pyramids were built of solid stone as tombs for their pharaohs.

Located in the West Bank, the Tower of Jericho is one of the earliest stone monuments in history.

Brain Builder!

Pharaoh Djoser's tomb was the first pyramid, near modern Cairo, Egypt. It is called the Step Pyramid.

Imhotep was the founder of Egyptian architecture. He was also a scribe, writer, priest, and doctor. He served as Pharaoh Djoser's advisor and designed the Step Pyramid.

The early buildings and towers were limited by building materials. Stone is heavy, and it's hard to get stone structures very high before they collapse under their own weight. Building techniques improved, but stairs higher than five stories were a problem.

Brain Builder!

Flying buttresses in the 1100s supported the roofs of Gothic churches so glass could be used in the walls. An arch attached to the building at the roof led the weight away from the building to a column of stone, which supported the weight. Notre Dame in Paris is a church that uses flying buttresses for support.

Notre Dame, in Paris, has endured destruction and subsequent restoration in many periods. However, much of the facade and interior still are true to the original designs.

Modern skyscrapers are quite different from early structures. They are no longer built of solid stone or mud bricks. The best design and engineering techniques available are used to construct new skyscrapers and towers. Elevators make taking a trip to the top a short, simple ride.

Buildings continue to exceed extraordinary heights. Currently, the tallest building in the world is the Burj Khalifa in Dubai, United Arab Emirates (UAE).

Not only is Burj Khalifa the world's tallest building, it has also broken two other impressive records: tallest structure, previously held by the KVLY-TV mast in Blanchard, North Dakota, and tallest free-standing structure, previously held by Toronto's CN Tower.

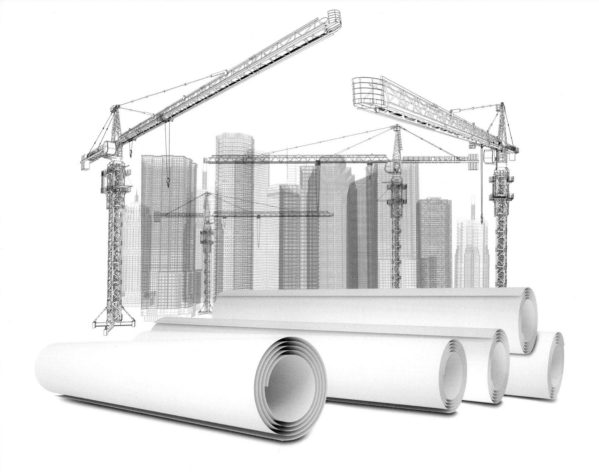

Powerful Forces

Constructing such tall structures requires a lot of planning. Engineers must make sure a skyscraper will be safe for people who live and work in it.

They must be **structurally sound** and able to hold the loads, or forces, placed on them. If not, the building will collapse.

Forces such as wind speed, gravity, and the weight of the building put pressure on it. These forces are the loads. The dead load is the weight of the building itself. This load doesn't change.

The live load is the weight of the people or items in a building, such as furniture, equipment, or anything that can be moved in or out.

Wind load, the force of wind on the building, can change, so it must be predicted.

Wind loads exert **torsion**, a twisting force. Think of wringing out a soaking wet towel, twisting out the water. Wind hitting a building on one side pushes against the building supports, moving them apart. On the other side, the supports compress. Strong winds can make towers twist so hard they buckle or collapse.

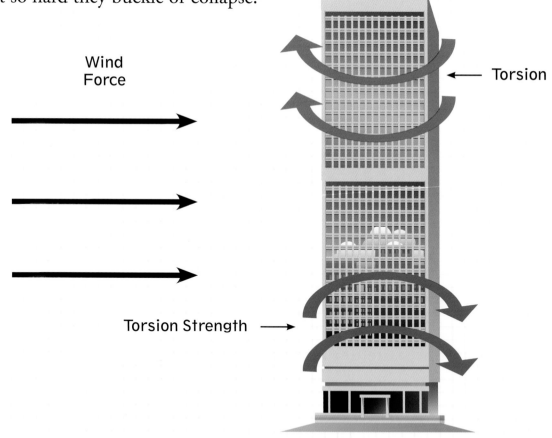

Wind Force

Torsion

Torsion Strength

Wind doesn't travel at the same speed constantly, so buildings must be designed to withstand the wind's turbulence and changing forces. Wind causes torsion, which causes shear stresses. A beam in torsion fails during shear because the molecules slide apart sideways. The beams can buckle and collapse if the building isn't strong enough.

Shear is a sliding force, much like the shears on a pair of scissors. Earthquakes may cause shear. They move one part of the building's support and make another section slip, causing a sliding motion. The building crumbles.

Gravity is a constant force of attraction between two bodies. Larger bodies exert more force than smaller ones. For example, the Earth is much larger than the tallest skyscraper.

The Earth exerts far more force on buildings than the buildings exert on it. Those forces must be accounted for so the building is stable.

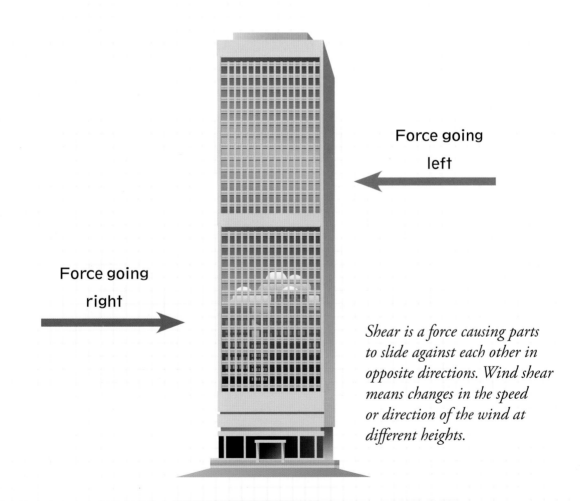

Force going left

Force going right

Shear is a force causing parts to slide against each other in opposite directions. Wind shear means changes in the speed or direction of the wind at different heights.

Brain Builder!

Sir Isaac Newton discovered that force is needed to change the speed or direction of something moving. The force of gravity moves outward from the object but it reduces over a distance. The Sun's gravity is strong enough to keep the planets in orbit but we don't notice it because it's so far away. The Moon's gravity has enough power to affect the tides of Earth's oceans.

Sir Isaac Newton
(1642–1727)

Eight planets orbit around the Sun: Mercury, Venus, Earth, Mars, Jupiter, Saturn, Uranus, and Neptune.

Compression and tension act on buildings to hold them up, or bring them down. Tension is a pulling force. It stretches something outward. Think of a rubber band. Pull it apart and it stretches. Continue pulling and finally it snaps.

Compression is a squeezing force. It presses things inward. A vise gripping two pieces of wood holds them together by compression.

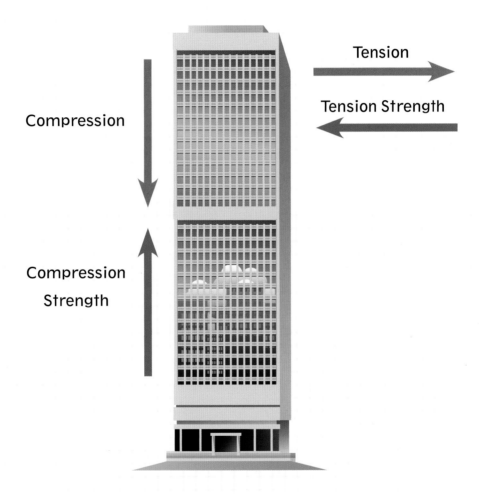

The upper floors of a building have less compression on them than the lower floors due to the weight of the building materials. With horizontal beams, there is more tension. The bottom of the beam stretches a bit more than the top, which is being compressed.

Deformation is another force that affects building design. When a material bends under stress but returns to its original form once the stress stops it shows elastic deformation. Too much deformation can cause a material to reach its limit, so after the stress is removed the material stays in its new shape. A permanent deformation is one that changes the shape forever.

Building materials expand and contract, too. As they warm up or cool down, the materials get bigger or smaller. Engineers take into account all of these forces and make sure structures can stand up to their effects. Architects use their engineering knowledge as they design a new building to make it both beautiful and safe.

Elastic Deformation

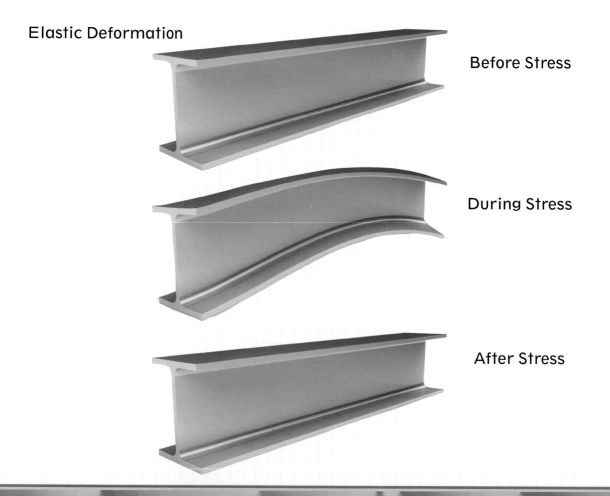

Before Stress

During Stress

After Stress

This foundation will soon be a skyscraper. As cities grow over time, vacant land becomes scarce and more costly. Skyscrapers are a solution for limited space, putting offices and homes in the air!

The Building Goes Up

A skyscraper can't stand up to the forces acting on it without a strong supporting foundation, or base. The foundation acts much like the roots of a tree supporting its trunk and branches. The ancient Egyptians made pyramids wider at the base than the top for support.

As buildings got taller, engineers had to figure out a way to support their heights. The foundations of modern skyscrapers go deep below ground to provide stable support.

Layers of soil, rock, and clay cover the underlying **bedrock**. Bedrock is the stable surface below soil.

Workers remove this upper layer of material by digging it out, making a pit. They often use heavy equipment to dig down to the bedrock. A deep base lowers the center of gravity of the structure, which is where the gravity is concentrated. This divides the building's weight evenly over the entire foundation.

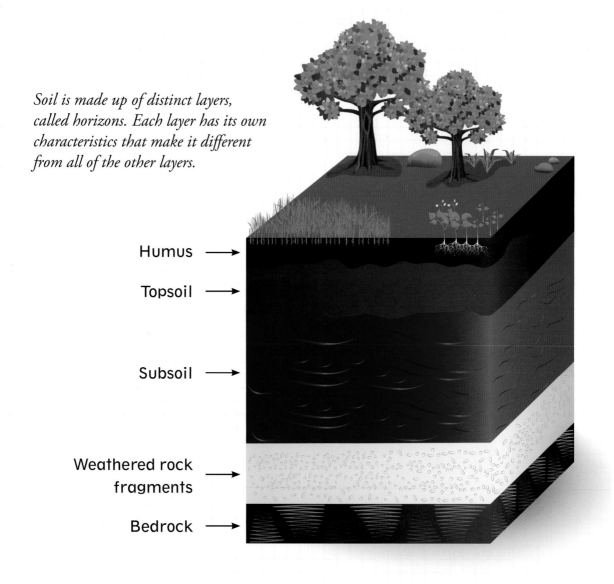

Soil is made up of distinct layers, called horizons. Each layer has its own characteristics that make it different from all of the other layers.

Humus →

Topsoil →

Subsoil →

Weathered rock fragments →

Bedrock →

Footings are drilled deep in the ground. They move the building load forces into the land. **Rebar**, reinforced steel, is laid down in the footings and concrete is poured over it to form reinforced concrete. The type of footing depends on the building's load.

Rebar also helps move the temperature around inside the concrete. This lessens the stresses produced by uneven temperatures and shrinking in the concrete.

Structural supports of different materials move the weight of the loads onto vertical concrete columns. These supports are often attached in the shape of grids or other designs. Structural supports are called by the shapes they form, such as I-beams or H-beams.

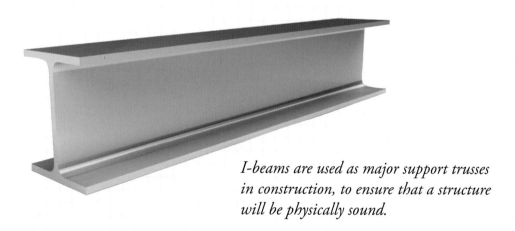

I-beams are used as major support trusses in construction, to ensure that a structure will be physically sound.

With a load on it, structural support beams flex and compress at the upper area. The lower supports are now under tension.

Columns of reinforced concrete are poured. The number of columns depends on the weight and size of the building and the kinds of materials used. Columns are part of the structural support. They also compress at the top and have tension at the bottom.

Sometimes concrete is poured around steel beams to make it even stronger. All the parts of the foundation make the **substructure**.

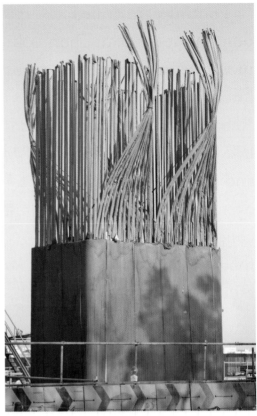

Reinforced concrete beam

This skyscraper foundation is in the early stages of construction. Once built, it will reach into the sky much like the building in the background.

Brain Builder!

Steel is made of an alloy of iron and carbon and small amounts of manganese, silicon, phosphorus, sulphur, and oxygen.

The superstructure is the rest of the building. A skeleton of the building goes up. Support columns of beams are connected and bolted or welded together. They are braced with cross bracing.

The core of the building is usually made from reinforced concrete, however, researchers are studying using a sandwich of steel beams filled with concrete. This core increases the strength of the building, helping it stand against wind and earthquakes.

Core of building

As the skeleton rises, the structural work goes on and upward. The work on the lower floors begins at the same time. Floor supports are placed into position. They are attached to the core and support beams. A decking is added to the floor.

The outside walls are added. They are not for support and can be materials such as glass or metal. They are attached to the building's framework and secured. The interior is finished and then decorated.

When installing outer walls, although strength is not the utmost concern, builders also consider several other things, including how to minimize material demands and how the walls will be insulated and air-sealed.

The Leaning Tower of Pisa was designed as a circular bell tower. It is constructed of white marble.

Historical Towers

The Leaning Tower of Pisa was built using the most advanced construction methods for the time. Its design included columns and arches, which is considered evidence of understanding loads and weight. The finished tower weighed 14,500 tons (13,154 metric tons).

The Tower of Pisa was built as a bell tower. It stood straight for five years, but was built on a region of compact clay. The foundation went only ten feet (three meters) deep. After the third floor was finished in 1178, the tower began to lean.

The clay base wasn't strong enough to support the tower. Its weight shifted toward the weakest place in the clay. Construction stopped. People hoped the soil base would settle and hold the tower.

There are seven bells located in the bell tower, all tuned to musical scales.

In 1272, four more floors were added. One side of these floors was built taller than the other to balance it, but it leaned even more.

In the 1800s, an Italian architect decided to show the base of the tower so people could admire it. He dug a section away from the base. The tower continued to lean.

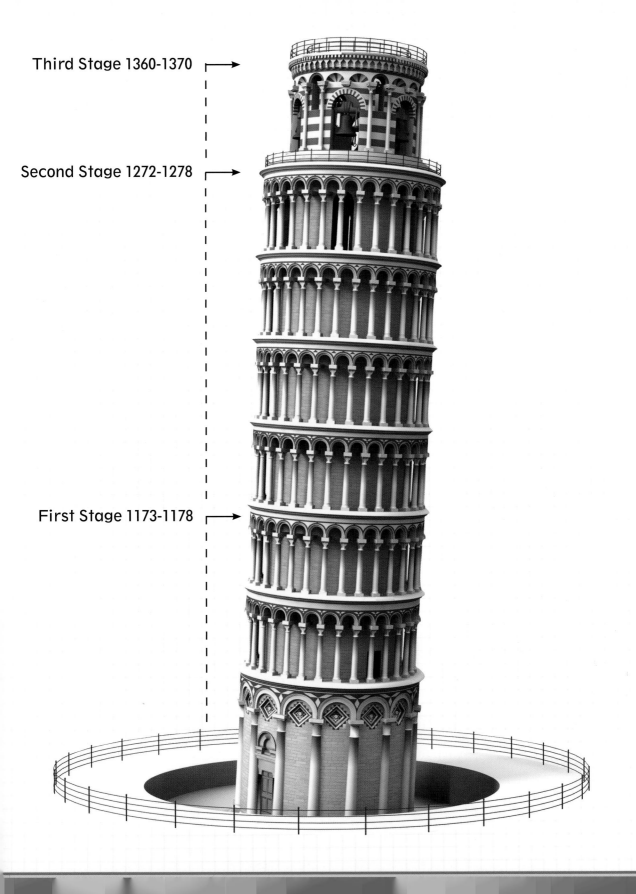

Third Stage 1360-1370

Second Stage 1272-1278

First Stage 1173-1178

During World War II, American troops were ordered to destroy buildings to reduce sniper threat. However, the Italians retreated before the United States army reached Pisa. The Leaning Tower was safe.

Italy asked for help to stabilize the tower in 1964. An 882 ton (800 metric ton) lead **counterweight** on the side opposite the lean helped balance it. In 1990, final work began to hold the tower. It reopened in 2001.

The Leaning Tower of Pisa was closed to the public in 1988 to prevent it from possibly elevating its inclination, but is now reopened to tourists.

Gustave Eiffel designed the Eiffel Tower in Paris, France, for the 1889 Exposition. This fair was to celebrate the 100th year of the French Revolution. The construction showed off the architecture and technology of the time.

Gustave Eiffel (1832–1923)

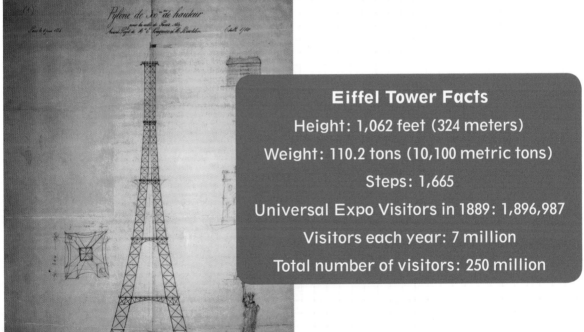

Eiffel Tower Facts

Height: 1,062 feet (324 meters)

Weight: 110.2 tons (10,100 metric tons)

Steps: 1,665

Universal Expo Visitors in 1889: 1,896,987

Visitors each year: 7 million

Total number of visitors: 250 million

Stephen Sauvestre was the main architect in charge of the Eiffel Tower. There were about 50 engineers, 100 iron workers and 121 workers involved in its construction.

The Eiffel Tower was meant to last just twenty years. Science experiments, including the first radio transmissions, saved it. It has been restored and refit as a tourist attraction. This important monument is a symbol of light and a visual symbol of France.

You can see around 37 miles (59 kilometers) from the top of the Eiffel Tower.

Massive skyscrapers need to rest on bedrock, the solid rock underneath the ground's soil, or they won't be able to stand up. At the World Trade Center site, the bedrock is between 55 feet and 80 feet (17-24 meters) down.

The World Trade Center Towers in New York City were built as a symbol of American commerce. Their location took special techniques to dig the foundation. The site was next to the Hudson River, so the pit flooded.

A three foot (one meter) trench was dug around the perimeter. Concrete was pumped in using forced water and a clay mixture to block and hold the water. This left a reinforced concrete watertight wall around the site. The perimeter footing needed 60 strong, load-bearing steel columns spaced close together on each building side.

Reinforced concrete and steel columns were used in the Twin Towers' construction. The finished buildings were completed on April 4, 1973. The North and South Towers were the tallest buildings in the world at that time.

On September 11, 2001, American Airlines Flight 11 struck the North Tower and United Airlines Flight 175 struck the South Tower. More than 25,000 people were evacuated, but both Towers collapsed. The attack and collapse killed 2,746 people.

The complex, located in the heart of New York City's downtown financial district, contained 13.4 million square feet (1.24 million square meters) of office space, almost four percent of Manhattan's entire office inventory.

The **debris** was cleared, but debate arose about what to do. Plans were set to create a memorial and museum on the site. The new building, One World Trade Center, is the tallest building in the United States. It is 1,776 feet (541 meters) tall. Architect David M. Childs designed the three million square foot (278,709 square meter) building.

One World Trade Center is a reminder of the horrible attacks of September 11th, but also a beacon of hope and strength to all Americans.

The new Tower, at first called the Freedom Tower, honors the Twin Towers. The square base is the same size as the original towers. The observation deck height and the glass **parapet** height are the same as those of the original towers.

Glass prisms cover the base, but there is a concrete wall designed to protect the building from blasts. The Memorial Museum opened September 11, 2011. One World Trade Center opened on November 14, 2014.

Each of the original World Trade Center Towers had 110 stories.

Brain Builder!

Fire safety is a concern in skyscraper design. The design of One World Trade Center included wider stairwells, refuge areas, and special elevators with water resistant controls inside smoke resistant areas.

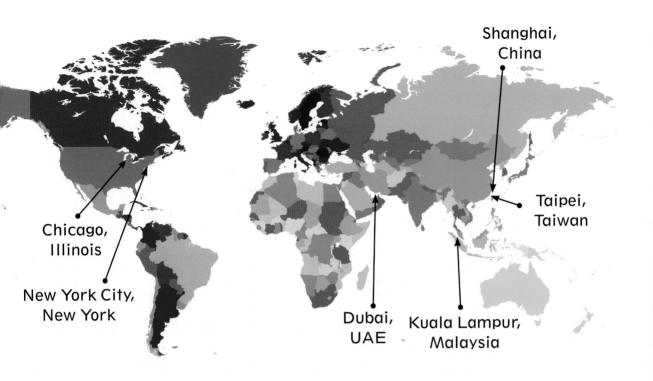

Shanghai,
China

Taipei,
Taiwan

Chicago,
Illinois

New York City,
New York

Dubai,
UAE

Kuala Lampur,
Malaysia

Towers around the World

At 2,717 feet (828 meters), the Burj Khalifa in Dubai, UAE, is currently the tallest building in the world. It is almost twice as tall as the Empire State Building. However, the Burj Khalifa is almost half its weight.

The Burj Khalifa holds the world's highest swimming pool and fountain. The world's fastest elevators inside it rush upward at 26 miles per hour (10 meters per second).

The building's design by American Adrian Smith is based on a native desert flower. A six-sided base supports the tower. It is designed to hold up against desert wind shear. The design begins with the Y-shape at the base and grows narrower as it rises.

One branch of the Y faces the wind. The wind breaks and slides around the other two wings of the Y. Each shape supports the other. The stepped towers contribute to wind resistance.

Adrian Smith's most inspiring muse was a regional desert flower, the Hymenocallis. Its harmonious structure is one of the organizing principles of the tower's design.

Hymenocallis

The Burj Khalifa is supported by a reinforced concrete mat. This sits on top of reinforced concrete building supports. The concrete mat is 12 feet (3.7 meters) thick. The outside covering is made of reflective, glazed glass panels. This shields the building from the desert heat and sunlight. Outside columns line the building for support.

The building's enormous weight is supported by 192 piles, or support columns, buried more than 164 feet (50 meters).

Shanghai World Finance Center (SWFC) in Shanghai, China, is also a skyscraper, standing 1,614 feet (492 meters) tall. SWFC uses three structural systems made of columns, beams, braces, a center core, and projecting beams for support. These help brace the building against earthquakes and high wind.

The Shanghai World Finance Center has the highest outdoor observation deck in the world and features the distinctive shape of a square prism, an ancient Chinese symbol for the Earth.

The Taipei 101 in Taipei, Taiwan, reaches 1,667 feet (508 meters) in height and has 101 floors. The steel and glass structure, shaped like a pagoda, is designed to stand up to typhoons and earthquakes.

The shape of the Taipei 101 resembles a bamboo shoot, a symbol of strength in China.

Brain Builder!

A pagoda is a tiered tower with many eaves.

The Petronas Towers in Kuala Lampur, Malaysia, are the tallest twin towers at 1,483 feet (452 meters).

There are 104 concrete supports with a thick raft foundation. The supports go from 200 feet to 374 feet (60 meters to 114 meters) deep.

The Petronas Towers were designed by architect Cesar Pelli.

The Petronas Towers are a backdrop for many Bollywood movies.

The floor plan is based on two rotated squares. This shape forms an eight pointed star used in Islamic art. The building's top gets smaller as it goes up. A skybridge connects the two towers at floors 41 and 42.

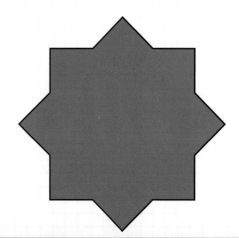

The Willis Tower, formerly named the Sears Tower, is easy to spot in the Chicago skyline. In 1969, the Sears Company needed a larger set of offices. The architecture firm of Skidmore, Owings, and Merrill designed a 110-floor building for them. It was the tallest building in the United States at the time.

In 1988, the company sold the building. It was renamed the Willis Tower in 2009.

At that time, a large renovation took place. A museum and observation bays of glass on floor 103 were added to make Skydeck Chicago. The glass bays stick out from the building 4.3 feet (1.3 meters) on all sides, including the top and bottom!

From the Willis Tower, you can see four states: Illinois, Indiana, Wisconsin, and Michigan.

Located in the center of New York City, the Empire State Building is one of the most recognizable buildings in its skyline. Built in 1931, the 102-floor skyscraper was the first building to have more than 100 floors. It took 3,400 workers to build it.

Brain Builder!

There are 1,860 steps from street level to the 102nd floor of the Empire State Building.

Depending on where you are, the skyscrapers around you may not make the world's tallest lists but they are still impressive. The Times Tower in Kenya, Africa, is a modern skyscraper with 38 floors. Though that may not sound very tall, it is the tallest building in all of Kenya. It is officially known as the New Central Bank Center and was completed in 2000.

The Times Tower won't be the tallest building in Kenya for long. The Hazina Trade Center in Kenya will be 39 floors. It is planned for completion by 2016.

What's New with Skyscrapers?

Architects and engineers want to save energy and reduce pollution in new skyscrapers. Today's tall buildings use lighter materials, reducing the weight of the structure.

Coated glass windows cut down on the heat from the sun. Double-paned glass helps insulate buildings. Radiant barriers, often made of aluminum, reflect light. Other kinds of insulation are made from newly developed materials, such as blue jeans or cellulose, a plant product.

Technology and improved construction methods allow skyscrapers to be built higher and higher. But, as they grow larger, new problems arise. These buildings require huge amounts of electricity.

Solar roofs and solar panels provide an alternative and pollution-free way to generate electricity. One World Trade Center is powered in part by twelve hydrogen fuel cells. The Willis Tower's renovation included a new power-generating glass that produces solar energy.

Skyscrapers are notoriously huge energy consumers. Getting building owners to reduce the carbon footprint of their massive buildings is one step toward conserving energy.

In Shanghai, the SWFC uses a zoned air-conditioning system. Also, multi-layered glass on outside windows helps maintain the building's temperature. The Estela de Luz, or Pillar of Light, in Mexico City has a double skin to filter air from outside and mix with air freshened from the green plants.

New York's One World Trade Center was built with a focus on **sustainable** design. It includes renewable energy, inside daylighting, reused rainwater, and recycling.

Shanghai World Finance Center (SWFC) in Shanghai, China.

Brain Builder!

The Willis Tower is home to peregrine falcons that hunt pigeons, a pest bird in Chicago. They nest on other buildings, but hunt prey at the Willis Tower.

Not all towers are steel. The Imagine Peace Tower in Iceland is formed of light beams reflected upward. The beams change as the weather and air conditions change. The Tower shines only at certain times of the year.

The Imagine Peace Tower is an outdoor work of art conceived by Yoko Ono in memory of John Lennon. It is situated on Viðey Island in Reykjavík, Iceland.

From skyscrapers that climb to incredible heights to towers made of light, what will engineers and architects think of next? What would you build to make your mark on a city skyline?

Timeline

Completion dates of major skyscrapers and towers:

1370	Leaning Tower of Pisa	(Pisa, Italy)
1889	Eiffel Tower	(Paris, France)
1931	Empire State Building	(New York City)
1972	World Trade Center North Tower	(New York City)
1973	World Trade Center South Tower	(New York City)
1973	Sears Tower (renamed Willis Tower)	(Chicago, Illinois)
1986	Lotus Temple	(Delhi, India)
1998	Petronas Towers	(Kuala Lampur, Malaysia)
1999	Jin Mao Tower	(Shanghai, China)
2003	Two International Finance Center	(Hong Kong)
2004	Taipei 101	(Taipei, Taiwan)
2007	Imagine Peace Tower	(Reykjavik, Iceland)
2008	Shanghai World Finance Center	(Shanghai, China)
2008	Burj Khalifa	(Dubai, United Arab Emirates)
2011	Estela de Luz	(Mexico City, Mexico)
2014	One World Trade Center	(New York City)

Glossary

bedrock (BED-rahk): the stable layer of earth that can support a structure's weight

counterweight (KOUN-tur-wate): a heavy support on the weak side to help balance a load

debris (duh-BREE): the pieces of a broken building or object

deformation (di-for-MAY-shuhn): a change in the shape of something

footings (FUT-ingz): the lowest part of a building's support system in the foundation

innovate (in-uh-VAYTE): develop a new idea or to a new way of doing something

parapet (PAIR-uh-pet): a low protective wall around a structure

rebar (REE-bahr): reinforced steel

shear (SHEER): a sliding force

structural supports (STRUHK-chur-uhl suh-PORTS): the parts of a building or structure designed to keep the building upright and stable

structurally sound (STRUHK-chur-uhl-lee SOUND): a building or structure that is able to hold its loads and stand up to the forces on it

substructure (SUHB-struhk-chur): the foundation or building part that is below ground

sustainable (suh-STAY-nuh-buhl): used in a way that doesn't completely remove resources

torsion (TOR-shuhn): a twisting force

Index

beams 13, 17, 18, 19, 20, 34, 44

engineers 6, 9, 14, 15, 41, 44

footings 17

forces 9, 11, 14, 15, 17

foundation 15, 16, 18, 22, 27, 36

gravity 9, 11, 12, 16

pyramids 6, 15

rebar 17

reinforced concrete 17, 18, 19, 27, 28, 33

skybridge 37

skyscrapers 5, 8, 15, 41, 42

structural supports 17

Show What You Know

1. Discuss the differences between building towers with stones and bricks and building towers with steel.
2. Which tall tower used the most advanced building style? Explain why.
3. Choose two buildings from the book and compare and contrast them.
4. What can we learn from studying ancient and historical buildings?
5. Design a skyscraper of your own and make a list of the ten most important features to be included in the design.

Website to Visit

legacy.mos.org/etf/force.html

www.pbs.org/wgbh/buildingbig/skyscraper/index.html

www.sciencekids.co.nz/engineering.html

About the Author

Shirley Duke likes visiting tall buildings and towers. Two of her favorite buildings were the Eiffel Tower and the Leaning Tower of Pisa. She climbed the steps of the Leaning Tower and looked out of the top. She learned that foundations are the most important part of a building.

Meet The Author!
www.meetREMauthors.com

www.rourkeeducationalmedia.com

PHOTO CREDITS: Cover © fazon1; title page © Luciano Mortula; page 4 © Lakov Kalinin, Krisztian Miklosy; page 5 © Icenardo; page 6 © Geothea, Andrews71; page 7 © Pillerss; page 8 © Ed Tellling Photography; page 9 © Cherezoff; page 10 © drmakkoy; page 12 © National Portrait Gallery; page 14 © 3dfoto; page 15 © radub85; page 16 © designua; page 17 © rihardzz; page 18 © askdreamstime, eldadcarin, nakorn; page 19 © Colly168; page 20 © nemalo; page 21 © Lukiyanova Natalia/frenta; page 22 © Paul Merrett; page 23 © 3DAgentur; page 24 © Rolf Gebhardt; page 25 © Felix Nador, Maurice Koechlin/Émile Nouguier; page 26 © vintagerobot; page 27 © Uerlman; page 28 © Dan Howell; page 29 © IndustryAndTravel; page 30 © Victor maschek, Haryadi CH; page 32 © dblight, MiaoMiao LV; page 33 DubaiResident 06; page 34 © Minh Tang; page 35 © Sean Pavone Photo, Noppakun Wiropart; page 36 ©Holger Mette; page 37 © shariffc; page 38 © Chris Pritchard; page 39 © Victorianl; page 40 © Charles Vowman/Corbis; page 41 © Denis Babenko; page 42 © dynasoar; page 43 © chungking, tvivbickis; page 44 © Brynjar Gauti2012

Edited by: Keli Sipperley

Cover and interior design by: Renee Brady

Library of Congress PCN Data

Skyscrapers and Towers / Shirley Duke
(Engineering Wonders)
  ISBN 978-1-63430-416-0 (hard cover)
  ISBN 978-1-63430-516-7 (soft cover)
  ISBN 978-1-63430-607-2 (e-Book)
Library of Congress Control Number: 2015931729

Printed in the United States of America, North Mankato, Minnesota

Also Available as:
ROURKE'S
e-Books